Scarlatti
for Guitar

Ten arrangements by
Peter Batchelar & Richard Wright

ABRSM

Published by ABRSM (Publishing) Ltd, a wholly owned subsidiary of ABRSM
© 2008 by The Associated Board of the Royal Schools of Music

Cover by Dahlia Designs, text setting by Adam Hay Studio.
Music origination by Andrew Jones.
Printed in England by Caligraving Ltd, Thetford, Norfolk.

Introduction

The son of opera-composer Alessandro, Domenico Scarlatti was born in Naples in 1685 and died in Madrid in 1757. After two years in Venice he settled in Rome, in 1709. His principal patron there was the exiled Polish queen, Maria Casimira, who ran an ostentatious musical court. Here Scarlatti would have encountered the lutenist Silvius Leopold Weiss, who, at the time, was in the service of her son Prince Alexander Sobieski.

In 1719 Scarlatti left Italy for a career in Portugal and Spain. He returned to Italy for a few years, during which his father died, but from 1729 spent the rest of his life in Spain. His music became increasingly infused with Spanish influences – indeed, Manuel de Falla would one day regard him as a compatriot. Of his 555 keyboard sonatas, nearly all were written for Princess Maria Barbara of Portugal (later Queen of Spain), his pupil and patron, and more than half, remarkably, during the last seven years of his life. No autograph manuscripts for the sonatas survive, but copies in Venice made for the Spanish queen are generally regarded as the most reliable source. These give just the barest essentials: slurs and staccatos are rare, and dynamics practically non-existent.

After the piano and harpsichord, the guitar is the instrument most often associated with Scarlatti. Indeed, Ralph Kirkpatrick, his biographer and the scholar responsible for cataloguing the sonatas, states that 'although Scarlatti never played the guitar, surely no composer fell more deeply under its spell'. Thus the guitar's open strings appear as pedal points in Scarlatti's music, and unexpected dissonances are created when harmonically unrelated chords are held against them. The often incomplete part-writing is also typical of the guitar, and Kirkpatrick describes Kp. 208, with its folksong-inspired long vocal lines, as 'courtly flamenco music'.

The present collection

The sonatas Kp. 34 and 94 are two of Scarlatti's earliest harpsichord pieces, composed before his arrival in Spain. They betray his Neapolitan origins through their sudden changes of thirds, switching between major and minor, and their chromatic alteration of anticipated intervals. Kp. 77, 80, 81, 83 and 88 also belong to an early group of sonatas, almost certainly conceived as pieces for a solo string-instrument plus continuo. They give few pointers to the startling originality of later works, but their simple bass lines make them suitable as intermediate-level guitar solos. Kp. 208, 292 and 322 are all genuine keyboard sonatas, but are close stylistically to the continuo-accompanied solo sonata. In the course of arranging these pieces, four were transposed. The original keys are: Kp. 34, D minor; Kp. 80, G major; Kp. 83, A major; and Kp. 94, F major.

Three types of ornaments are found in these arrangements: appoggiaturas, mordents and trills. In the case of appoggiaturas, the small notes are held for their written value, subtracted from the note they precede. Thus the small notes in Kp. 322 are performed as quavers, entirely, and those in the Minuetto of Kp. 77 as semiquavers. The type of slur between the small note and main note indicates how an appoggiatura is to be played. When this is a solid line, both notes should be played with the right hand; when dashed, a left-hand slur is intended. The mordents, in Kp. 292 and 77, begin on the upper note; where preceded by an appoggiatura, the appoggiatura acts as an elongated upper note. For trills and selected mordents, full realizations are given at the bottom of the page.

Peter Batchelar & Richard Wright, 2008

Sonata Kp. 80

Sonata Kp. 88

Minuetto ($\flat$ = *c*.116)

Sonata Kp. 34

Sonata Kp. 94

Sonata Kp. 81

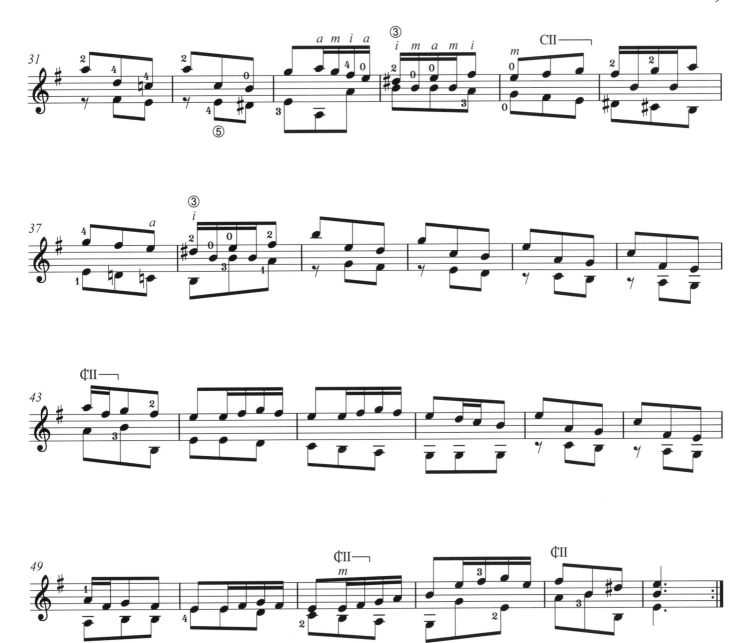

Sonata Kp. 208

Andante cantabile ($\quad = c.46$)

6

(a)    (b)

Sonata Kp. 83

Sonata Kp. 292

Sonata Kp. 322

Sonata Kp. 77

Minuetto ($\flat$ = c.120)

11:16